When We Were Young
& other poems

Patricia Spicer

Wooded Hill Press
Eugene, OR

When We Were Young
and other poems

Cover Art by Stephen McMillan

Book cover design, interior design,
and publication management
Eva Long /www.longonbooks.com

All the Dawn's Composed of Flowers

All the dawn's composed of flowers,
  Effused the rose, the sky deranged,
A rainbow-colored sea of hours,
  The pure profile of earth is changed.

I'll conjure luxury from the noon,
  Rubies and emeralds from the sun,
Summon Ishtar with a rune
  Form her dusky Babylon.

Dear Possible, in orbéd light
  From the heart's translucent core
A masque of beauty and delight
  Brims the golden Eastern shore.

~ Stephen Mann Thomas (1932-1961)

Contents

SEASONS

VALEDICTIONS

I. Commentaries

When We Were Young

When we were young we were so serious,
pressing the campus hillside with our weight;
when the names of Kant or Plato crossed our tongues,
we thought they made our small conclusions great.

There lay the waiting world and here sat we,
eager to take up either sword or pen
to set her wrongs to right, no uncertainty
except the time to act—what greatness then!

Now we return to find grass under brick
where springs ago we rhetoricians lay.
Now we agree, as earnest students pass,
that life is short and the air seems cold for May.

Reunion

Strange to see her now with eyes
that look from such enormous distance,
a look blunted by too much seeing.

I remember when her look leaped into space
without fear of falling,
tumbled unbruised like an October leaf,
when her voice was an unlearned song
and her hands wove a poem.

Now her eyes are cautious
like a looker around corners;
her voice mocks the old song, being flat,
and her gestures are a tedious paragraph
on the human condition.

I would almost cry, "This is not my friend.
This is a different being, a stranger!"

But through the change I know her well,
for still, as long ago, she mirrors me.

Carving

When you carve a figure from a block,
you have to cut away, the sculptor said,
everything the wanted form is not
and so may lose more than you save.
And as you gouge it bite by bite,
what's thrown away must equally be right.

Just so a seeker given massive choice,
must cut away life's greater needless mass,
cast chips and shavings from a steady hand,
must choose exactly what to keep and where
to make a smooth coherent line—
Though the result be spare, so that it please,
though it be small, so that it shine.

Returning Home

There is a will in man to journey home,
to seek out his beginning at the end.
Every mountain, valley, desert must be sweet
to someone standing Janus-like in middle years,
pondering the compass points of birth and death,
dreaming to close the pathway of his life
in one coherent curve, the spawning salmon's race
to reach his own predestined ancient place.

Now no one dies in the house where he was born,
or returns to the hillsides where he used to play,
for the very earth they loved is torn away,
and temples that gave comfort to their souls
are in some strangers' hands—who see
no treasure there, but only ancient art,
the pillaged treasure of commodity.

In the name of home we killed in ancient days
to keep the hungry strangers out, but on they came.
We fled to other lands, seized other fields,
and used or sold them like some passing game.
Breaking rock to gravel, soil to dust, tree to ash,
we killed the earth we could not learn to love,
and here we stay to perish where we must,
having lost our old inheritance of place
like prodigals who can't return to grace.

There Was a Time

There was a time when chairs were made too tall,
or I too small, my legs too short,
my feet suspended just above the floor.
I sat on cushions when we dined;
whenever I asked questions, I sensed that grown-up
answers were reserved or incomplete.
And all the time I thought, "Someday I'll grow—
These things were made for bigger guys than me;
someday I'll fit the world and then I'll know."

Well, now I sit on chairs whose legs and mine
both reach the floor, no stretching up
to see above a window sill or gate;
but still I see a world I cannot reach,
not even now, can never reach, too high, too wide
for any child of man, however grown in years,
for as I grow, its boundaries extend—
a world that few know what to ask,
and if it answers, none can comprehend.

I Heard Two Men

I heard two men discuss theology
as if it were something more than words,
as if it were a doorway into God,
as if God were a country they could map,

or a puppeteer who held the world on strings
and only they could see beyond the veil
sufficiently to tell the way He made things move—
and only they dared comment on His mystery.

When men mold God with trowels of verbiage,
plaster with metaphors and lexicons of terms,
then fix it all in laminated creeds,
they reduce a living tree to fiberboard.

I wonder now what sort of deity
could give fig for their theology.

There Is a God

There is a god, but he is not divine;
he labors at his canvas every day,
drawing lines with light and gravity and time.
Sometimes he picks up one of us to make a stroke
or takes a human tribe to build a minaret.
Sometimes he sits and ponders, smiling,
frowning over shading or design.
Sometimes he paints out a mistake,
since every artist knows the need for change.

There is a god, but he is not divine;
a little vain, he changes robes with every dawn
and turns before the mirrors of his light, in stars
and seas and dewdrops and the bloom of clouds;
he plays with drumming water like a child,
blows up a mountain now and then to see the lava
run like glowing dragons, writhing in the night.
He scatters birds—and worlds—
and blows the pinwheels of the galaxies.

If god were truly wise, as theologians say,
I might not know he sometimes feels regret
that everything will end that he has made,
as he idles in a flowered dell in spring
or walks along the ridge at end of day
and marvels at his own far-seeded stars.

Prayer

If god exists, there is no need to pray;
I am a thing that god already knows—
How could I be more known,
no matter what I have to say,
no matter what the thought I shape to words?

If there's a god, what reverence could I add
to adulations sung by centuries of saints?
Psalms and chants and dances stamped in sand,
cries from minarets that God is Great—
all this I know he knows. It is enough.

If there's a god, what would I ask?
that I, a snail, might run or fly?
For me the world is simply flat;
to ask god for a change is to imply
the world could be improved in this or that,
and I have yet know it as it is.

If there's a god, my prayers are fallen leaves,
a needless scatter on a holy wind;
IF there's a god…but if there's not,
Then these same leaves fall purposeless and rot.

That Force

That force, First Cause, Big Bang of energy—
did it contain some deep defining plan?
Did it weave a purpose in exploding light
as it set loose its bright stampede of stars?

Did it foresee in uttering its forging Word
that words could serve to dazzle and conceal
whenever truth is craven to desire?
Did it know that love, the crucial bond of men,
could bend its loop to trammel and betray,
as craftsmen bend a yew into a yoke
or hunters weave a willow to a cage?

Did it know all this—or was Creation merely blind
as it unfolded newer worlds, while earth grew small
and smaller in its wake—and vanished from its mind?

The Ballad of Human Bones

Here is a pile of human bones—
Come, tell us if you know how,
which were humble, which were proud,
which died believing in his god
and which went hopeless to the sod,
or does it matter now?

Here is a pile of human bones—
Come, tell us if you know how,
which had a love, a wife, a child,
which wielded pens instead of arms,
which tilled the fields on blasted farms—
or does it matter now?

Here is a pile of human bones—
Come, tell us if you know how,
which was a youth on his way to school,
which was his teacher, which his friend,
which turned on him at the violent end,
or does it matter now?

Take crosses, crescents, doubled stars
to scatter like seeds behind the plow;
though some will hit, some miss the mark,
like land mines planted in the dark—
It doesn't matter now.

Pan

Pan was not at first a god of woods and wilds—
In ancient times he walked the hills and fields,
companion to the shepherds and their flocks.
He taught them how to weave slow lonely hours
with singing reeds and garland summer flowers;
he frightened wolves away with stamping feet,
protected drinking sheep at the river's bend,
showed men where the lambing ewes were hid.
All this Pan did, who was the shepherds' friend.

It seems one day—no one recounts the time—
Pan found a wolfling orphaned in a den
and took it to the men for pity's sake;
they gave it sheep's milk, bones, and firelight;
it grew into their pack and followed them.

When Pan returned the shepherds scoffed at him:
"We do not need you anymore—we have a dog."

Apollo and Cassandra

Cassandra spurning Apollo's love, though love
for love she had preferred to give, spoke thus:
"You gods! you pompous striders of eternity!
How well have mortal women learned your ways,
breeding your half-immortal sons who walk the sky
while you and they leave earth-bound mothers,
alone and desolate, to die. Brief love,
betrayal await. Sweet Daphne, dryad, knew.
We are the cup you drain and set aside,
a fading taste on insatiable young lips,
forever young—forever old—it doesn't matter which.
They cannot love indeed who cannot die!"

Phoebus, before he was consumed with wounded pride,
fell silent for a time and turning his perfect head aside
so that Cassandra might not hear his almost human
sigh
or see in his gray eyes that he was stung,
as to himself he said, "My love is brief
because I too am victim of mortality,
unable to stand by and watch you die so young."

Delphi

Who made this crumbled place?
Who hauled and set these massive stones,
Now scattered like thrown dice?
Why here in such a steep redoubt?
Chilled in winter or sun-beaten like the moon,
a rocky, winding way for pilgrims' feet;
Greece has a thousand crags where foolish men
might spend their strength to wrestle stones
against their weight and chisel them
into unnatural forms. Why here?

What use is this to me? Why did I come to see
a shrine that lived and died a thousand years ago,
its back against a giant limestone cliff,
piled and unpiled by trudging men and mules?
Who cares where Zeus's eagles may have met,
or what victory some stele celebrates,
who won the Pythian games some vanished year?

Of what importance is all that to me?
Yet here I stand in a nest of knotted hills,
right of Parnassus, left of the gleaming sea,
And here, here where I stand
stood Laios first, then Oedipus his son,
and Pindar chanting his commissioned odes,
and pious Plutarch intoning ancient rites,

and Hadrian weeping for Antinoos,
and busy old Pausanias making notes,
and matricidal Nero marking down his share
of bronze and marble for the ships to Rome.

Yet here I also stand, a puny stranger in a holy place
and feel the wind of landing eagles on my face.

Mycenae

I have seen the stones of Mycenae,
ten, twenty, a hundred tons apiece:
I have walked on the stones of Mycenae
like an ant on the face of a fallen king.

I ask the stones if they have a life in death,
whether their shadows hold processions
and echo the bleat of sacrificial goats.
Do they dream of the folded plain they sleep upon,
full of horses and heroes and slaves and gold?

These stones were shaped by human pride,
raised up by the tyrant will of kings.
What did they care for the sandaled feet
of a girl going down to her marriage at Aulis,
or the pacing of a mother who plotted her revenge
in their cold and secret corners?

They took no notice whatever of two children,
a brother and sister, perched on their bone-hard summit,
looking out to an imagined fleet of ships,
far, far beyond the dusty herds below them,
vision clouded with longing for their father,
whose sanguine return from war was well foreseen,
and when he fell they continued to weep unnoticed.
Even then those stones were indifferent to mourning;
they answered only to earthquakes and armies
and the repeated plunders of robbers and time.
They never knew that anyone else was here.

Like a Perfect Circle

Like a perfect circle or the axle of a wheel,
all human minds contain some notion of ideals,
some image of a guiltless happiness,
a lover's endless love, a painter's masterpiece,
a haunting glimpse of beauty, wisdom, truth,
a kingly ruler, uncorrupt and wise—
the pedestal that shames our failed resolves
And makes us think we have imagined god.

Although it differs in detail, all men retain
some version of this paradigm. All understand
there is a scale of value somewhere in the mind
without which human hopes would not exist
and human acts would all be purposeless.

These measures must be bonded in the bone,
derived through volvox and amphibian;
this is the balance at the core of life,
the cycles of the moon, the seasons' turn,
the right and left of hands and fins and wings;
and though we scorn this knowledge as mythology,
we are the seed of Gaia and the sky,
and in the clutter of our mere mortality
we carry the genetic sign of gods.

No One Would Guess

No one would guess, coming from another galaxy,
that while we thump our drums and twang our strings,
spin on highways,
screech through skies,
chatter and blather
and mill in malls,
like porkers penned in holding sties,
we noisy gabblers hold a noiseless place inside.

No one would guess that tucked in spaces in the din,
squeezed and sandwiched in the Babel's tower,
there is a cluttered but inviolate room
where we retreat to cry or meditate,
pester the Silent Answerer with "Why's,"
brood on our revenge or fate,
spar with fear,
encourage hope,
in the only place we have to hide,
and though the world beats on the door,
no one can guess at the anxious soul inside.

This we concede. Yet men whom we call wise
have looked at treading donkeys,
bleating sheep, hawks and peacocks,
elephants and flies,
pronounced on what's inside and what is not,
and solemnly declare that only Man has thought.

Love in the Nursing Home

The wife of the man in 203
comes every day to satisfy her mind
that in the darkness of dependency
his bed is dry, his aides are close at hand.
Diverting as she can the spite of time,
she brings clean clothes and hangs them as at home,
fills up his glass and sets the pillows straight,
reads from the paper, feeds the man his meal,
sweeps off the crumbs and pats the drool away.

When the day is warm she takes him for a walk;
pushing his chair, she chirrups with the birds.
"Look at the poppies, dear! oh, aren't they nice?"
She hovers, folds his lap robe, pats his hand.
He murmurs some. His words are pebbly sounds;
his random gestures make no shape at all,
and when she goes he slumps into his chair,
bent like melted candle in the entry hall.

Then Molly Miller comes, tugging her wheels along,
unkempt and gray and furtive-eyed,
with bright crochet concealing ragged bones,
giving no sign what she is thinking of.
He reaches out and speaks in vibrant tones:
"Oh Molly, sweetheart! You're my only love!"

Vagrants

Sauntering in the lanes of afternoon,
we pause to watch a line of earnest ants
carry tufted seeds to storage in their granary
or bustling outward on their way to gather more—
Then one, then two or three begin to fray
the stringent cordon of the common track
and wander off among the bracken stems—
as tall to them as pillared trees to us.

Are they some foragers sent out to bring
the precious news of provender back home?
or merely stragglers from the troop whose sensors
somehow failed and so they lost the way? Would they
return at last or stray forever into uselessness?
Cut from the mass, are they the same as dead?

My friend and I, below the redwood boughs,
adrift in patterned light and shade,
are we some roving foragers of thought
who hope to find the source of soul's content
to carry back and tell our hectic tribe?
Or are we merely lost, bewildered and inept,
useless, until we find the flow of men again
and rejoin the unseen power of the line?

Strange

Strange how we perceive the touch of things
in ways we do not feel with hand or eye—
how spatters of rainfall make a flood
of hope or fear inside a waiting mind,
how light refraction turns to color
in the sight, and sight to beauty or disgust;
Strange how a touch or glance may turn to love
or hate, a single word to hope or to despair.
Vibrations of song bring inward smiles—or tears,
A distant voice excites replies—or flight.
Someone or something absent turns to pain—
How strange! when there is nothing there.

Strange how the senses are like fertile soil—
a touch to them is something like a seed
that roots and flowers instantly in mind.
A thought, mere thought, which no one weighs
or sees or calculates, is beautiful or cruel.
A thought divides the world and recreates it
in that different mode we call significance,
for what is sensed is not what something means.

I know. I know from everything, but most of all
from you. Your touch was always light,
your face mere image in my eyes, your voice a sound.
No touch required me to love, no loss to grieve.
How strange, before I could be quite aware
of what I did, I turned these jottings of experience
to joy, remembrance, and despair.

Time

Time, run your course for me because I know
your perfect mastery. I cannot even call
my days my own; my seasons and my hours grow
from you. Indeed, Time, you are all.

You are remembered pleasure, light of hope,
rollick of festivals, the special joy of days
when nothing special happens, the westward slope
of afternoon, the rising moon's reflected rays

shed down the months you make. You are
the pain of loss, the sleeplessness of night
when guilt has made an eye of every star
and I feel the inquisition of their sight.

You are the union of existing things—
fern and flower, gull and ocean, horse and hill,
everything that changes, dances, hobbles, springs,
or hovers on its pinions, seeming still.

You are all that. But your life is borrowed too,
as mine from you, so yours from timelessness.
I'll rest in you at last, but you yourself will die
somewhere beyond eternity's abyss.

Festival

There is a festival tonight—
The guests are coming, a la mode;
the table's laid, the room is bright;
the host and hostess greet and smile—
"You're Patrick's cousin, is that right?"
"Poor Julian has driven miles!"

They all partake hors d'oeuvres and wine;
the bluffer bores, the vamp beguiles;
the dipsomaniac feels fine;
a date (or jewel) is someone's pride
to slow-parade around the room,
and everyone takes lies in stride.

The more they talk, the more I cringe,
the more they laugh, the more I shrink;
this party is a verbal binge,
and yet I see the cause—I think.
Through the windowpane the night is wide,
and we all deny the dark outside.

Night People

Don't let them say—
crossing a street scarred with neon,
accompanied by a fanfare of motors and horns—
"This is the night,"
this stretched, tormented, artificial day,
this clack of feet and wheels and passengers
that bears no likeness to the living dark.

Night people are reserved, attentive, still,
admiring scarves of moonlight in the trees,
lovers of the nuanced world of owls,
of fireflies and whispers in a pool
where hidden fish make dotted circles flower,
where air is an unwritten treble clef
strung with the cicadas' courtship song,
and the sky is spattered with resplendent stars;
night people hold their breath before this subtlety
of sight and sound, head cocked, expectant,
isolated in the sea of life's first being,
worshipers before the dawn of gods.

A Leaf

Today I dropped a leaf into the stream,
where it lingered on its touching point
like a bead on a mirror, stem curved in the air,
waiting as if for the moment bewildered,
being disjoined from the link of its nurture.

Then it began to revolve in a current,
subtle as morning exchanging for moonlight;
It turned on its axis, its invisible center,
then described a revolving and stately ellipse,
moving outward a little and inward a little,
turning and going and coming and turning,
while the uplifting edges seemed to wave goodbye.

I see it departing, my tentative missive,
frail and unsure of the end of its journey—
a leaf grown and loosened and set in the current,
a leaf or a verse, unique and yet common,
turning and flowing among leaves, among verses,
whispered responses, lost in the riffles,
bearing a secret—this one is my own.

Sunday

Our Sunday was benign,
requiring no tiresome decisions;
there are no messages or mail,
the telephone sleeps bat-like in its nest;
the day flows on in soft-repeated riffles,
so gentle, harmless, full of trifling chores,
small leisured outings, easy smiles.

It creates a certain liberality of mind
that ends with earnest prayer—
that they may be content who work this day.
God ease their weariness and more—
console the people we have labored through
the week to keep or render poor.

The Haters

Where is it? we whisper muttering on the street
in the roaring din of the human condition;
Where shall we look? we worry aloud, not knowing
what we say because our very thoughts are drowned.

Together and separately probing we search
through single rooms of faded-draped hotels
or mass-produced apartments, in crowds, in multitudes,
so hungry to discover that the stomach curls with pain.

Because the hope we had that either god or man
would find us lovable—if we but reached for love—
became a hand reflected in a glass, we reached no more;
we found no grace, and works were spent in vain.

And so we search instead for that which struck
strikes back, for even the hand of hate may steady steps,
and spite will give a strong, if rasping rope to hold
in a sea that floods us with our lack of specialness.

The thing we seek may go by any name—
In the end whoever finds it finds the same
relief, the welcome enemy—the Blame.

Shadows

When I wake in the morning and see
the first faint line of gray where darkness
fails along the eastern ridge,
and far off trees arise like spires,
I think of dawn as a royal procession,
full of pennants and cheering and song.

I think of common duties and light chores,
a friend to visit, a garden to tend;
I think of hot coffee and oranges
and a sweet breakfast pastry.
And the morning flows around me
like water that laps a Mediterranean island,
soft chanting and pink with adventure,
and my day is full of flowery nooks.

But below the hilltop's line I see a shadow;
I see someone waking, already exhausted,
dragging himself to a stinging cane field,
or dragging herself to a maquiladora;
I see the day is on them wringing hot
and the fanfare that guilds their procession
is scourging voices and rasping machinery.
I see no breakfast whatsoever
and feel the knotting of urgent stomachs
and minds that would be filled with rage

if there were room inside their bleak despair.
I see no softly lapping water,
but an endless course of galley oars,
their handles slick with sweat and grief.
Will this day ever end? Will it ever!?
Only in tomorrow's grave.

I turn away, comfortable, bland, secure,
searching to find excuses for my kind—
no, not my kind—my class.
We are the ignorant who wave degrees
and sneer or shrug and sagely pass.

A Juror Ruminates in Court

Here they examine error trapped in time
like a micro-organism on a slide,
declare the allegation of crime
against the state, and here they set aside
all moments past except that reckless hour
that waited like a trench across the road;
All other facts and actions lose their power
except the ones entangled by the code.

Here eddies and meanders change their course;
the short is lengthened and the long cut short,
for every word takes on a different force
when diverted through the corridors of court.
Who could foretell—most certainly not he—
that a day that dawned like any other day
would sweep the accused to this calamity,
like a flood that tears a leaning tree away?

Who could foretell we would be sitting here,
impaneled to observe, evaluate
whether a witness has his story clear,
might misremember or prevaricate—
judge human lives that we will never know
except in this bizarre, disjointed way
in which a partial view is put on show
and legal tactics win or lose the day.

The judge explains that pity has no place,
and the defendant is on trial, the law is not;
to judge a human past the reach of grace
is the single labor fallen to our lot.

We jurymen whose lives are laced with error,
but somehow have escaped from error's cost,
must view that rapid with a certain terror
in which one of ourselves might have been lost.

To judge the drowning from our rocky bluff—
the credentials of good fortune are enough.

Evolution

What a burden ancient priests imposed
on man, God's chosen creature, special friend,
so many rules to codify and keep,
such real estate to manage and defend!
So much depended on God's seneschal—
The power to move mountains or to slay,
entrusted to a beast, which after all,
was not much wiser than the wind at play.
So many ways to flounder and go wrong
and wreck the world he was to regulate—
How lucky man had words as well as song
to make excuses and prevaricate!

It was at last too much for man to bear,
as hard to manage as the gift of wine;
Thank God, He let geologists declare
man's origin might not be quite divine.
Darwin and Huxley both explained the plan
as work of chance and skill and appetite,
that what became a frog was just as right
and fit to live as what became a man.
Now we should all be overjoyed to find
that birds are just as crucial as mankind
and quadrupeds are cousins to us all—
denial of which resulted in our fall.
But unsharing man preferring to walk blind,
evolution will roll flat and leave behind.

Rain — Matthew 5:45

—In the heart of the lotus, he said,
 eternity and time are indistinct;
 peace breathes in the there that is here,
 and the Buddha descends in love like rain.—
 I smiled at the earnest old man.
—If you don't take cover you will die,
 I said, and he smiled back.
 We sat awhile. I searched the sky for planes.
 He watched the clouds.
 He said the cycle of the seed was man
 and would grow up again,
 new rice in ancient fields.

Planes came and passed us overhead,
 making thunder beyond the hostile ridge.
 The old man stood and searched the sky again—
 The summer storm is very close, he said.
 I will take cover now.
 And slowly he walked away along the path;
 not watching, I felt him go and went beside,
 while the broad leaves struck
 began their ancient dance;
 there in the forest I met my enemy
 and found his face was also wet with rain.

To a Sleeping Child

Watching as you perfect lie,
I see you with a troubled eye;
as you climb the years, though mountain high,
you'll have no better fate than I
for you will laugh, but also cry,
and you will love and you will die.

Saltillo

In the plaza in Saltillo, by the cathedral there,
the big bells' toll is pounding the wispless air.
Through the thunder a dizzy buzzing, crooked and thin—
the old blind beggar goes on playing his violin.

Stars

Every night I walk to the feet of the stars
and ask the old unanswerable questions:

Who or what force first set you afire—
massive cauldrons of being—and why?
Why did you turn water, light, and stone
into a womb of flowers and flesh?
And why did you let us come to eat your world
like some poor living beast aswarm with ants?
You cannot make too many galaxies or spawn
too many spheres, who have infinity to fill,
space on space beyond all systems, powers, light;
though creatures die, you cannot think of death,
too busy burning, turning in creations' wheel.

Some say you rule our fate, but I think you only stand,
distant, detached from the trouble you have caused;
a mother who has no arms to hold, no heart to care,
a judge whose law is carved in rock and bone.
Unmoved by prayers, regret or good intent,
you will not, cannot save our earth from death,
but who will mourn her loss if you will not?

Why do I ask and ask again, always unanswered
as I am, bowed by the silence of the stars?

Beauty

I believe that beauty will return,
that winds will sing more complex choruses
when the lyres of the pines retrieve the slopes
and rivers, having overcome their dams
and escaped from their canals, will shout delight.
Birds will flood the air again in spreading waves;
swallows and swans and hummingbirds will flow;
deer and lions will return, not friend or foe,
but hunter and hunted as they were before,
with place enough to lurk or hide or run;
roads will fill with rivulets of grass
in jagged cracks. Rubble will swarm with mice
and nesting birds, and hunting snakes
will slide mellifluous between the blocks;
soft owls will doze among old broken beams.

Beauty will return through patient years,
a little at a time, in tessellated bits;
the deserts will shrink back from reaching rain,
the weary soil embed slow-delving roots
to bind the slashes left by plow and axe;
flowers will dazzle when April has no name,
and the sun will crimson seas unmarked on maps
when no calendars enumerate the days.

Beauty will come back but when she comes,
she will hear no voice to sing— as poets did
when poets walked the earth—her praise.

My Land, My Patria

This is my land—the land where I was born;
these are my cradling hills of oak and pine;
this is my river where the bracelet waves
of light encircle leaping fish and herons' legs;
this is the source of all that I call mine.

This is my land that sleeps below the moon,
lulled by the whir of bats and croon of owls.
My patria never sleeps, but gorges constantly
on convoluted deals and strategies
and power plays, digesting in its bowels.

And so my patria grows fatter every day—
in towers and in tunnels built by men
who quarrel in chambers, quibbles in the courts,
who sow and reap in gold, but not with seed
that grows to fruit—to offer seed again.

My land is thirsty for her giving water,
lonely for oaks whose nesting birds have fled,
since my patria has torn her forests down,
stopped her gliding rivers with concrete
and traded starlight for a neon crown.

That crown is such a tawdry recompense
for beauty bartered. I don't understand—
these people with their talk of patria,
who deal their ugly pillage like a prize—
did they never have a land?

Do I See

Do I see a light ahead in darkening dusk?
Is that the shore I once set out to find,
a passage that I booked so long ago
I can't recall the goal I had in mind?

That odd thing is I feel my life has strayed,
although I have forgot what trip I planned,
a stranger stranded on a foreign ship
that makes its way to quite a different land.

It seems my passport has been lost
or else expired, but still this vessel goes
while I lean on the rail, confused and tired,
certain this port is not the one I chose.

Searching

Searching through the world of night and day,
unguided by a plan and wearied out,
I am the predator and the prey,
forever stalking Hope and feeling Doubt.

Whenever I come along the cooked way
upon the joy I leap to seize, then
doubt transforms the image into clay,
and gray despair bays at my heels again.

Like a hawk that instinct hurtles high,
far, far from its paternal nest,
lured by the flow of the endless sky,
the hunter cannot find a place to rest,

and though the world is deep and wide,
the hunted cannot find a place to hide.

When I Tell My Dog

When I tell my dog that I love her,
she doesn't ask if it's platonic,
fraternal, maternal, romantic,
how much do I love her, how long will it last,
or whether I've loved someone other before.

She doesn't protest that a dog is unworthy,
or complain of genetic, historic dependence,
doesn't question my motives or emotional needs;
she suggest no quid-pro-quo of equal weight,
expects no verbal or written agreements,
containing descriptions of duties and rights.

When I tell my dog that I love her,
she seems to assume it's true,
and that is the reason I tell her—
and the reason I don't tell you.

Worms

It warmly rained for several days
until the worms at last were driven from
their soggy paths to curl and wriggle on the walk.

If any one of them had thought—
this too will pass—
it could not know the rain would cease,
the walk would freeze,
and it would turn to glass.

When I was young I used to state
that man controlled some small
selected corner of his fate;
but I've lived to see, now I am grown,
that the world of worms is not
so very different from our own.

A Cloud

When I die I think I will become a cloud;
each day my form would change to suit my mood—
expansive, thunderous, resolved,
or small, contemplative, and mild,
hurried some days and streaming with the wind,
on other days content to doze
in the hollow of a hill or on a mountain slope,
the backdrop for a rising kite or hawk.

Rain I would love to give, in deserts most of all,
wake flowers from a monochrome of dust,
surprise a farmer mournful in his field,
give voice to threading falls
and fluted tunes to torpid summer streams,
revive a pond for thirsty deer or fox,
refresh the delving roots of gasping trees,
and give a butterfly one silver drop to sip.

Above the hills, above the smoke of noise,
I would go silent towards the stars,
to levels where their light is dazzling clear,
and spend my nights admiring the moon,
and be her screen or scarf or trailing veil
when she should choose to drape her nakedness.
The thought of death brings more regret than fear,
the loss of poetry and song, the things I love—
but if I cannot read a verse again,
then I would be a verse to someone else

who just by chance would see my poetry
made visible in golden morning light,
or rose and crimson in the fine reflected
harmonies of dusk, and turning to another say
(or only to himself alone) "Look up!"

Traveler

Here under the paling dome of an autumn sky,
the sun just stepped below the hill,
the raked clouds spreading high and white,
I am a traveler who takes along
these clouds and this descending light,
carefully packed in image and in thought.

A traveler at dusk who still holds onto morning,
carries each season, each stop on the way,
every star, every moonrise,
every love, every stranger,
farmlands and cities, valleys and hills,
like a magical fisher whose close-knotted net
takes minnows and mermaids in its catch.

A traveler draws everything into his being,
draws it the way that a canyon draws water;
yet he doesn't grow into monstrosity or vanish
under mounds of clutter, but smaller and lighter
like a sigh of nostalgia,
or a song born from sorrow,
a distillation of worlds.

We Who Live

We who live our lives by rods and rulers,
take right turns at clocks and calendars,
form rigid lines for flags and festivals,
chop hills and meadows into tidy squares,
cut curving oaks to make flat planks and beams
and rescue rivers from the curse of bends—

"Forward!" we cry, to claim our destiny,
ignoring the calm succession of the seed
that in cycled seasons turns from root
to stem, to branch, to bloom, to mulch,
unhampered by a sense of self or goal,
unmindful of man's desperate linear time,
laying down spent leaves for later seeds—
as we might better lay our words, our deeds.

II. SEASONS

Sunrise on the Beach

I watch the full moon, paling, fall to sea
beyond the surge where rocks are ground to sand.

Above the waves a sea bird whitely gleams,
  alight with dawn, while all the heaving sea is gray below.

I see dark strands of kelp like random wreaths,
while on the bluff the pines are etched in gold.

And suddenly the moon has washed away
in the soundless turning tide of coming day.

October's End

October was my friend. She sang in me—
I floated in her air, swam in her sea,
day after day so soft, so warm, so one—
as petal is to flower, earth to sun,
figure and ground in the study of each other—
that's how I loved October and she my lover.

One evening a cold wind blew from the north,
making the dry twigs crackle and the branches cry,
and searching for October, split the sky,
and shook her fragile figure back and forth.
Her gown of golden leaves, shed in her flight,
was all I found in pale November light.

Crickets

September evening finds the setting sun
pulling from the ridge its last display;
the crickets' chirping has just now begun
to fill the silence left by wearied day;
all across the dark the crickets spread
their evening song that floats me out of time
to other autumn nights I had thought dead,
when crickets filled the stubbled fields with rhyme.

Their chirping pulls me back across the years
to a distant village newly come alight;
as I look homeward through the glint of tears,
I see a country house with conjured sight
and hear the cricket songs so thickly flung
from the golden fields I loved when I was young.

March

On mornings when the year begins to turn
like a furrow newly cut for sowing hay,
when the season seems to balance on its edge,
and one touch of wind could tip it either way—

On mornings when the larks lift from the meadow
on black and yellow wings of shade and sun,
when tall clouds reach up to the washed heavens,
and new foals stagger up and run—

Then we forget the endless night of winter
as if that dreary time had never been
but a dark dream we awakening have forgotten,
erased by flowing crocus once again.

Year after year spring is the reason why
we still insist on loving things that die.

Rain at Night

Deep in the night the rain brings sweet relief
and music to earth's silent thirstiness;
each droplet finds its own tympanic leaf,
and passing wind in trees gives lull or stress
to steady beats. Lying warm in bed,
with windows wide, I wake to euphony
of water falling, falling, freely shed,
priceless life to grass, to trees, to me—
sweet softness of the rain, redeeming sound!
A blessedness beyond necessity,
it beats a peaceful beauty, striking ground
in antiphonal irregularity;
throughout the night, awash in its refrain,
I lie awake and listen to the rain.

It's Winter

It's winter now. The sun rests on his elbow
above the southern hills as if not quite inclined
to stand erect and do his daily work.
At first we feel refreshed by lower light
and dance like trees wrapped up in autumn wind,
whirling off their dusty faded leaves.

At night we gather by the fireside
to turn and sip a flickering glass of wine,
retelling tales of spring and harvest time;
then by and by we feel the ancient fear
of all mankind, for the sun has slipped away;
as if by sympathetic magic we cajole;
hanging lights on windows, rafters, trees,
burning candles at our pagan feasts, imploring his return.

It's winter now—brief day, long night
fold into one another with low slanted bars;
Dawn veils herself in cloud, the sunset sneaks away;
we wait and hover now, encased in cold
where only piquant stars and cracking frost are bright.

Change

When I wander underneath the eaves of oaks,
I curse the worms that shred the budding leaves,
though they gain strength by carnage to exchange
their many-legged voracity for wings.

And the wind that strokes the grass across the hill—
that pliant green of April's natural lawn—
will burn it beige before the end of June.
There spiders weaving in the parched remains
conceal themselves in rivulets of web
to reap some thirsty flutterer's mistake.

And when the soaring hawk turns easy arcs,
then almost I forget, suspended by his wing,
that this same predator will be time's prey
and his keen eyes will feed some sightless thing.

And I, observing, am myself observed
by time's own agent, searing leaves of grass.
The pain, the fear, the wonder, and the joy
I carry to this place—these too will pass.

Indian Summer

I didn't see the leaves begin to go—
It seemed that summer lingered in the air
until one day I walked across the hills
and saw the trees were bare.

It seems the branches now are only bones,
lacking the robes that gave their structure grace,
but then I see them spread against the sky,
and look! the trees are lace!

November Wind

The sun goes early, early down—
cold wind assaults the silhouetted trees,
swirls up and twists the bat-black leaves,
which gathered up and whirled again,
are spread like flocking gulls along a beach.

Cold wind has blown the moonlight half away
and scattered stars across the fields of space;
their sharpened points are cold with frost,
and the pallid daylight on the western rim
is blown to ash and lost.

Return

Through softened air I see cool autumn's fond
return in Ceres' golden footsteps on the hill,
and Bacchus walking vineyards with his wand,
strike the leaves aflame with morning chill.

Can these enduring gods remind us who
we are, so entangled in our long mistakes
that in our lust for doctrine overthrew
the natural wonder that right worship takes?

Now let old gods of earth return again
from cave and hill and stream and grove
and cover all our childish cries of "Sin!"
in fragrant garlands blessed with holy love.

Then all the rhythms of the world will be reborn
when fair-tressed muses wake us from our trance.
Then saints and martyrs will forget their scorn
and join the nymphs and satyrs in their dance.

Summer Solstice

Pausing on the distant hill, with radiant eyes
he turns on the world his look of soft regret
and spreads the darkening rim with golden sight—
Phoebus, my lord, hold back. Do not go yet!

All summer I have watched you climb the hill,
aiming towards your northern-most ascent,
where this one day you reach the highest ridge
and touch the peak where summer's length is bent.

The peak will seem bereft when you are gone,
but patient under winter's coming night—
as we should be, anticipating dawn,
and another summer at its glowing height.

Dawn

If excess is a sin (and I agree it is),
then when the dawn came robed in rose,
and dropped her veils like Salome
in layered scarves of amber, blue, and red,
and dazzled on the eastern hills
in nakedness no waking eye could doubt,
then all the blushing world could see
the goodness of iniquity.

Under the Moon

The trees have spread their blankets on the ground,
and the arbor lays its stenciled lattice-work
in clear repeated squares of dark and bright,
like woven forms in intricate design.

Everywhere the white moon presses down
flattens the fields like liquid stone,
buries the world in borrowed light,
self-satisfied, as if it were her own.

Moonscape

This is a night when moonlight tarries late,
trailing her luminescence in her wake;
now like a parting guest she turns to smile,
lingering by the door with one who stands inside,
wanting to prolong their fading festival a while.

Parting? Meeting? It is hard to say—
The moon looks back into a face we cannot see,
standing beyond a sill of mountains gone to gray,
and all the sky is plated oyster pearl
and it is neither night nor day.

The Fog Is In

The fog is in tonight, but the air is bright
under the hidden presence of the moon;
the meadow is mysteriously white
that wears a mottled green in daylight's noon.
Fog darkens day, but now is light-infused,
for the moon reflected in each drifting mite
of mist is mirror-magnified, diffused,
and fills the air with layered scrims of light.

I won't suppose they have no skill to show
whose simple duty is the droplets' place
of filling up the air with what small glow
each can reflect of the moon's compelling grace.
Although it is the only art they know,
they serve the light—as a poet does also.

There Is a Spider

There is a spider that weaves a basket web
low in the grass—to reap an errant gnat;
both web and spider are so delicate
it's difficult to see where they are at.

But when I walk in early morning mist
across the fields, I see their myriad strands
dew-glinting like transparent crystal flowers,
blooming in the tangled grassy stands.

The silvered web may spoil the spider's catch
and so disarm its practical intent,
but for myself, I see a field of glass,
a hundred goblets where the light is bent.

For them the threads are threads, but what I see
in slanted morning light is poetry.

Lizard

Lizard, I've known you ever since I was a child,
but I used to shiver because of your quickness
and because other children said you could poison—
"Blue-belly! blue-belly!" they cried as they scattered
out of the threat of that miniature dragon.

Lizard, now I stop to watch your watching me
with needle eyes, half-curious, half-wild.
Now I see your scales in rows of beige and blue,
running your length in perfect parallel.
I know you do the most amazing things—
how you flatten yourself in slits between the rocks,
how you run like an arrow, jump like a rainbow,
how you hear a wispy fly with folded ears—
how you master a wall with your fingers of thread.
I admire the way you tread your world,
and like your skin my childish fear is shed.

Companion

When I move the moon moves with me,
watching me through the scattered branches
of an oak, racing me along the meadow's edge.
Am I mad to call her my companion,
as personal to me as my own thought,
when I know she follows everyone the same
and whispers the same entwining secrets
in the blooming scent of night?

And does she dance for me, for me alone,
on the rippling mirror of a hidden pond,
and does the music of the stars arrive
at last from space, pursuing their swift light,
to lend her dancing its unearthly grace?

Am I absurd to say the moon is mine
when she and I are standing face to face?

Trees at Christmas

The cadavers of the trees are hung with lights,
gaudy at the wake that is their own;
I'd rather walk the coldly moon-struck night
to see the trees alive and hung with stars.

But I dishonor them by finding fault—
they are a perfect sacrifice to god,
the Sol Invictus to whose birth and death
their birth and death show reverence.

This is no Jewish prophet's natal feast—
before the Jews, Egyptians, Greeks and more,
in huts and caves men feared the dying light
and prayed and danced the sun to life again
and wooed him with a tree—as we do now.

Tracks

Up and out before the break of day,
I stroll in fog across the low-tide beach,
where pricked in sand I see the night's display
of crossing tracks above the breakers' reach—
the four-foot marks of skunk, raccoon and deer,
and between the foam and scrambled seaweed vines
the dainty fans of peeps and gulls are clear,
like prints of leaves laid out in crisscross lines.

When I glance behind and see the hardened toe
and heel I leave, then I regret the trace
of the broken contract that my footsteps show,
and I take off my shoes, as in a holy place,
to merge my prints with other mortal kind,
bare-footed, for the rising sun to find.

Iris

You
Vaunting, flaunting,
Curling, curving question—
(Eternal brevity of splendor)
Am I in April? asking
Lily flower
Fleur de lis
Iris
Iris
You

III. Valedictions

Death

Death, you ruin everything. Strange
how you can have such overweening greed—
that you must own whatever knows the change
of growth, holding every egg and seed,
marked in the private grounds of your estate,
how you decide with your unswerving eye
to gather one in bud and for another wait
until the fruit is full, the ears head-high,
or over-grown perhaps, collapsed and dry,
or festered with the maggots of decay
until that rotting thing may long to die.
By which I see how through extending days
I may yet lose my rage and at the end
look up at your dark shape and call you friend.

I Wonder

To which of us has death been more unjust?—
I wonder by the grave where you were laid,
since my own youth is mingled with your dust,
buried with vows that in our spring we made
without a thought of winter's chilling gust.
All gleams of summer darken in this shade;
only a longing, years divorced from lust
trembles alive, which death cannot degrade.

Each day lies under night's returning thrust;
each season joins the former in parade
that winds its way to final peace—we trust—
when very part of us has sunk, decayed.
For now my longing waits though death denies
its watch. How long, I wonder, till my longing
dies?

Meeting Death

I'd never met with Death, not face to face,
but only heard of him or read in print
about his raging through some foreign place.
To me he was no more than winter's hint,
snatching off dry leaves in his embrace.

Death caught a neighbor while I was away
at school, too youth-distracted to attend,
and then my father's brother. Thus his sway
came circling in. He stole a childhood friend
who, careless, stepped into his path one day.

But still I never met him face to face
or guessed the endless grief he justified,
until he pushed you from your wonted place
and walked forever after at my side.

The World Has Ended

Closing the door I walk out on the street
and see to my surprise that cars still run,
that people clatter up and down with moving feet
and moving mouths, and buses swallow and disgorge
their human loads, and dogs trot past and sniff
and urinate, and babies cry, and telephones
rest expectant in their carriers,
and malls receive the press of those who buy,
while clerks look on with eyes unseeing,
standing there with selling hands extended,
and no one seems to know or care, no, not one being
that the world has ended.

I note to my surprise that the sun turns in the sky—
or the earth turns if you will. It must be turning,
since shadows on the sidewalk dwindle down, bend,
and stretch again under air that warms and cools,
as though the machinery that we know as time
still worked, each nut and bolt in place.
Night comes at last, and still to my surprise
Venus, as ignorant as all the rest, rises in the west,
not knowing that the day is finally through
in which time stopped, and, but for me,
it seemed that no one knew.

We Moved Mind-Bonded

We moved mind-bonded through love's synergy,
twining our lives in closely twisted skein,
turning with timely arcs like birds in flight,
finding secluded woodlands to reveal our pain,
pressed warm together in the shelter of the night.

One day you left my tracing turn behind.
The sky was red—I could not see to fly;
you plummeted while I flew onward, blind,
and to my wailing call made no reply—
the only time you ever were unkind.

Some starless night I'll lie again beside you,
though nevermore to fold each other in,
entangled in the weaving roots of cypress—
but then as if we two had never been.

Questions

So you are dead, and to my private shame
I can't recall…have twenty years gone by?
Perhaps because the sorrow is the same
as when you died, I am still asking, "Why?"
I miss your hand, I miss your earnest voice,
our strolls together at the end of day.
I want you here—but would it be your choice
if death had not so kidnapped you away?
We might have quarreled and parted like the rest;
we might have been as separate as we are…
How can I know if love would stand the test
with one more distant now than any star?
I have one question yet—and past relief—
Will my memory of joy outlast my grief?

What Dies, Dies Once

What dies, dies once—
After the funeral is over,
after the bleak box has been lowered
and all have gone but a few calm flowers,
there's a sense of relief almost in sorrow
for the worst has happened.

What dies, die once—
but human sorrow is immortal,
As leaves fall down and grow to fall again,
as one sunset grays on another's ashes,
as the dawn is a wound healing
to be again wounded.

We Climbed the Hill

We climbed the hill at sunset hand in hand—
The stubbled fields of oat and barley grass
seemed to descend beneath our steps, and there,
high on the bluff above the summer plain,
our faces cool in the whisk of evening air—
we stopped and gazed. I felt you close to me.

A crucible of clouds the lake below,
pale pink and darker rose afloat on gray;
the hills turned pale in the ebbing afterglow
that spread the sky like ripples on a bay.

Such flooding beauty must have made us numb
to fear, and the gentle cricket-humming air
lulled us to think that evening would not go,
and the cold night after would not dare to come.

A Dusty Book

Today I opened a dusty book and saw
with a flash that shivered through my hands,
an inscription to myself—with love—from you.
My memory murmurs, rousing from its sleep;
Can it be you ever lived?
It seems so long since that real life was spent!
But in the lamp your shadow over mine is bent
in another house where I am the lady now;
a trembling recognition shakes the page awry
between your hand and mine. The memory does not die,
though it may sleep sometimes like summer under snow;
your square script called me as I read,
shaking my youth awake. How could it seem
that you were ever dead?

There's So Much Pain

There's so much pain in grasping beauty,
so much foolishness in love—
Why couldn't I have let your beauty pass,
once having touched your being slightly
like moon on water, dew on grass?
If I had held you loosely, lightly,
my wounded hands would not have suffered so;
I could have written briefly, brightly,
then turned a painless page and let you go.

Starlight
(for Virginia)

The star that pierces through the veil of dusk—
distinct as mountain pinnacles glow white—
inspires song and verse and seaman's trust
and all who use—or simply love—its light.
Light years ago that star has died in space,
decayed as all things die because they must.
It's blackened cinders flail as cosmic dust.
Yet no star dies without its blazing trace
of rushing light, its signature of fire
that crosses galaxies in quantum waves.
Like stars, no treasured lives will quite expire,
but flow around the deception of their graves.
So friend, I have not ceased to see your face,
still imaged in the starlight of your grace.

Elegy in San Francisco

The sun has gone.
Where the city is, artificial day comes on,
and over the restless water
flowing out on either side where winding
lines of lights weave city-bent
or homeward from the ever-smiling strife,
the darkness glides.

Pleasure seekers jostle to their labor now;
the tick of goblets touching,
the click of the cup set in the saucer;
the blowing paper on the sidewalk crackles;
over the rung of the bar stool the brush of a suede heel
is hooked casually.

And yet a silence lies on every sound,
stops every meaning that comes from moving lips,
blocks cheerful glasses, cheerless traffic roar—
My love is dead and all I hear tonight
is the absence of a voice.

Arboretum

The arboretum smells of summertime;
indulgent sunshine strokes the velvet rose
and shines the waxy leaves of orange and lime,
and speckles earth where lacy cedar grows.
I lean upon one elbow on the lawn;
you read "The Book of Merlin," sitting near—
how Arthur blessed his kingdom in the dawn,
while faithful hedgehog listened like a tear.
The sight of Arthur's pain was all too clear;
here glowing lilies, like the stars, stood still,
and while you read I listened like a tear
to see that double image on the hill:
but as I blinked I found the vision cleft—
The King was gone and only hedgehog left.

Fidelity

When you died I thought I wouldn't love again,
but would always keep that emptiness apart,
which only showed how ignorant I was
of the clinging burr we call the human heart.

I guess I've loved a dozen times since then—
some more, some less, some almost not at all,
like a drifting twig that catches in a steam
and then tears on in the pelting rains of fall.

But as I climb the pathways of my life
and see my turnings from each higher hill,
I find without volition of my own
to keep my faith, that I have kept it still.

As when an old and weary emigrant
yearns home in heart to vanished towns and farms,
I really have no choice except to turn
to the well-remembered homeland of your arms.

Around me foreign ways and words abound
that I have learned to grasp the meaning of,
but no one sings the songs I learned in youth
in the flowing, sunlit language of our love.

Irony

It seems ironic now that when you died
you left it to so poor an artist
as myself to paint your portrait as memorial,
too poor a mason to engrave a single stone,
too poor a singer to complete your broken song,
and yet you left this task to me alone.

It's not your fault, of course—
This task to which I am inadequate
falls to me from fate's outrageous flaw,
whose blind unfolding always did equate
the great and small without a hint of sense.
While others master art, I bind my brushes
to a donkey's tail for art's pretense.

Since praising as I wish is past my power,
I must content myself with what all men
do best—complain into the heartless air
that you are dead and I am lacking skill
to even tell the world how much I care.

For a Lover Who Died Young

You would laugh if you could see me now,
twenty-five years further down the road.
What happened to the fragile girl you loved?
Gone to gray and wrinkles and a failing chin.
I wonder, would you know me if we met,
if we were introduced at some event,
and I was fifty and you still twenty-five?

Would you be puzzled if we paused to talk,
and I confused the things we shared with later years—
events and friends, and even lovers, yes,
and would you think, "This boring woman
turns my ear to stone. I wonder who invited her?"

Would we agree on common goals again?
Your eagerness for life would make me wince;
you always were intense to learn and do,
while now I potter in my garden, break for tea
and no longer quite expect to get things done;
if I achieve a row of broccoli I am content.
You took a hammer and a chisel to the block
of marble that you saw as life
and meant to carve it to its finest form—
and might have done…

…but we kissed goodbye one morning casually,
and coming home that afternoon, you died
and that was that.

But something still remains the same for me,
each time I stoop to put a flower on your grave—
the same impassioned joy I had in hope
when we were young, I hold in recollection now;
and at this striking point of wishing and regret,
we still might know each other in the light
and briefly clasp like old friends newly met.

We Cannot Know

We cannot know the living as the dead
since life itself intrudes new information,
busy and captious, ebbing and flowing,
full of unexpected turns and labyrinths.

But death encapsulates
and you can change no more, my love;
Having gone, you cannot go.
You have become my favorite study,
the book I read and read again
till I have it memorized.
I can look at you forever,
walk around you like a Phidian Apollo,
view every bone and muscle
in the image of my mind,
tie up a varied soul in recollection,
like a novel gone to press
or a painting signed.

I might accept such neat finality—
except I cannot change my least mistake
or set the smallest secret in your ear,
or kiss your perfectly remembered lips awake.

For Iris Anzilotti

You were always up by sunrise,
out in the orchard picking pears,
or in your garden harvesting
tomatoes, onions, cabbage, beans,
then into the kitchen with pots and jars,
putting up pickles, chutney, jam,
relish, ristras, garlic braids.

Now fall has come gain. The purple grapes
are waiting on the vines beyond your door;
I see the pickers stooping down the rows
when the clean September morning stands ajar.

But your deft hands don't wield the knife today,
startling the spiders in their shaded lairs.
The meadowlarks must wonder where you are,
whose daily song was a duet with theirs.

When you, the picker, are yourself cut down,
what fruit is there without a bitter taste,
blighting the sweetness in the reapers' bin?
But you would say, "Don't grieve. Be glad!
Go out into the fields. The sun is up again!"

Possessions
(for my mother)

The possessions you collected were almost
a part of you, the way possessions tend to be,
like leaves to trees, trellised vines—
letters, pictures, clippings, recipes,
knickknacks, vases, handmade quilts.
"Do you have my china?" you used to ask.
"Where is the bible my mother gave to me?
My paisley dress, my raincoat and my boots,
that box of silver napkin rings and spoons?"
Yes, where has all this gathering gone
now that you lie helpless in your bed,
past use or touch of recollected things?

Time is a storm of snatching claws,
flinging away all ties extraneous,
down to heart and head and bone;
Yet loss reveals your human essences,
and lines reform in ever clearer shapes.
When the chaff is gone the kernel is revealed,
gleaming like a gem, a lamp, a star,
a gentle spirit stripped of all façade,
still burning in the shrine of who you are.

I'll Know

Don't change with death, my sweet external world;
keep green your April leaves, as she last saw them green,
and the climbing rose in yellow-orange array;
keep lilacs and the curving iris blooms,
and do not brush your daffodils away.

Let the same old friends come through the door
and trade their common pleasantries
and time-worn jokes and old remembered tales,
the ones she loved to hear—or tell,
along with proverbs from her peasant past.
The many hands that make work light
can also help to make illusion last.

If the world's routine keeps its familiar form,
I can pretend it holds the thing inside,
only shut from sight a while, like linen stored,
not lost, not gone. While outer shapes remain,
I can pretend for now that what I do not see
is just one room or telephone away.
But if the jonquils fade and grass grows brown
and ivory buckeye candles fade and go—
not time, but change, takes her away from me,
almost unfelt, the stealing is so slow..
And so one day before I grant them notice,
the swirling leaves will tangle round my feet,
and above my head the naked boughs will show,
and though the fall be beautiful,
it will be change—
and I will know.

I Went to Greece

Dear Mother, when you died I fled to Greece,
as though to lose your death among the hills
or let the sea winds blow the pain away;
I went to Greece, where you had never been.
But in that land I saw your face again,
for its beauty lay, not in its skin, but bone,
in craggy hills almost bereft of flesh,
carved and hardened by experience and toil,
stripped by time of everything but strength.

Yet in attenuated soil life gathered still
(for it was spring) and flowers found their way,
creeping between the limestone slabs to dance,
and ancient olive trees and cypress spears
kept faith like proverbs, seasonless and true.
In everything I looked at I saw you.

And the sea was like your sighs of weariness;
its waves that bore the voyager through storms
have borne you to a tranquil port at last;
you disembarked, I stay on board a while—
until some other fate or purpose brings me in.

Dear Mother, when you died I fled to Greece,
but I found you there again.

For Dorothy Dunlap Tolpegin

Passing your house I see your flowers in bloom;
the lilacs and the roses mingle there
and crowd the walk till there is little room,
but now I think no walker comes to care.

The padlocked entrance hovers like a tomb
behind the step you will not tread again;
I marvel spring has had the heart to come,
knowing you aren't there to ask her in.

The Mourners

Crows perch on wire, their delicately
curled claws insulated; their beaks
gaping, give out a rasping cry.

They nod and chat and chafe until they tire,
then shedding a flurry of shadows on the ground,
they fly away to line another wire.

The Missing

The early rising sun prepares the scene—
strides up behind the hill and thrusts his hands
among the ragged clouds—now spent of storm,
spreads morning colors on the fields in green
and gold and shades of deep marine and mirrors
clouds in remnant pools of rain. The cattle toss
their tails and the hunting hawks trace ovals
on the sky, afloat on outspread wings;
the stage is set and all its cast is shown,
but the audience is one who sits alone.

I swallow down a sigh for those who missed
this pageant of a storm gone by. I pass the list
in mind, deplore their infidelity to life,
the vibrant friends who promised to live long
and yet died young. But still their broken vows
cannot dispel the silver glint on dotted lakes
or wrest the peace from field and grazing herd,
but beg me drink the scene for all their sakes.
I here incorporate the moment and the place
to mingle with the memory of each missing face,
and redeem their promise from inconstancy.

May some remembering friend—when I am dead—
watching the sky break blue after the storm is fled,
breathe its spellbinding show (as I do now) for me.

ACKNOWLEDGMENTS

Many thanks to my husband, Bill, for his
encouragement and technical assistance,
both necessities.

Thanks to the talented artist, Stephen McMillan,
who kindly gave his permission to use his etching
"Oak Forest" to grac the cover of this book.

Thanks also, to my extraordinary reader and critic
Jerry Parker, who must have been born loving
poetry and knowing how to spell.

More than thanks to my book designer and friend,
Eva Long.